EVERYDAY ENGINEERING

Roller Coasters

by Chris Bowman

BELLWETHER MEDIA • MINNEAPOLIS, MN

BLASTOFF!
2
READERS

Note to Librarians, Teachers, and Parents:

Blastoff! Readers are carefully developed by literacy experts and combine standards-based content with developmentally appropriate text.

Level 1 provides the most support through repetition of high-frequency words, light text, predictable sentence patterns, and strong visual support.

Level 2 offers early readers a bit more challenge through varied simple sentences, increased text load, and less repetition of high-frequency words.

Level 3 advances early-fluent readers toward fluency through increased text and concept load, less reliance on visuals, longer sentences, and more literary language.

Level 4 builds reading stamina by providing more text per page, increased use of punctuation, greater variation in sentence patterns, and increasingly challenging vocabulary.

Level 5 encourages children to move from "learning to read" to "reading to learn" by providing even more text, varied writing styles, and less familiar topics.

Whichever book is right for your reader, Blastoff! Readers are the perfect books to build confidence and encourage a love of reading that will last a lifetime!

This edition first published in 2019 by Bellwether Media, Inc.

No part of this publication may be reproduced in whole or in part without written permission of the publisher. For information regarding permission, write to Bellwether Media, Inc., Attention: Permissions Department, 6012 Blue Circle Drive, Minnetonka, MN 55343.

Library of Congress Cataloging-in-Publication Data

Names: Bowman, Chris, 1990- author.
Title: Roller Coasters / by Chris Bowman.
Description: Minneapolis, MN : Bellwether Media, Inc., 2019. | Series: Blastoff! Readers. Everyday Engineering | Includes bibliographical references and index. | Audience: Age 5-8. | Audience: K to Grade 3.
Identifiers: LCCN 2018000222 (print) | LCCN 2018000880 (ebook) | ISBN 9781626178243 (hardcover : alk. paper) | ISBN 9781681035659 (ebook)
Subjects: LCSH: Roller coasters–Design and construction–Juvenile literature. | Engineering–Juvenile literature.
Classification: LCC GV1860.R64 (ebook) | LCC GV1860.R64 B68 2019 (print) | DDC 791.06/8–dc23
LC record available at https://lccn.loc.gov/2018000222

Editor: Paige V. Polinsky   Designer: Jeffrey Kollock

Printed in the United States of America, North Mankato, MN

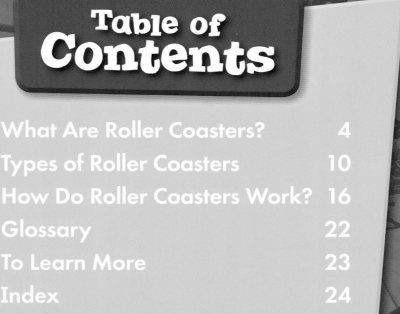

Table of
Contents

What Are Roller Coasters?

Roller coasters are thrilling rides. They have steep railways and fast cars.

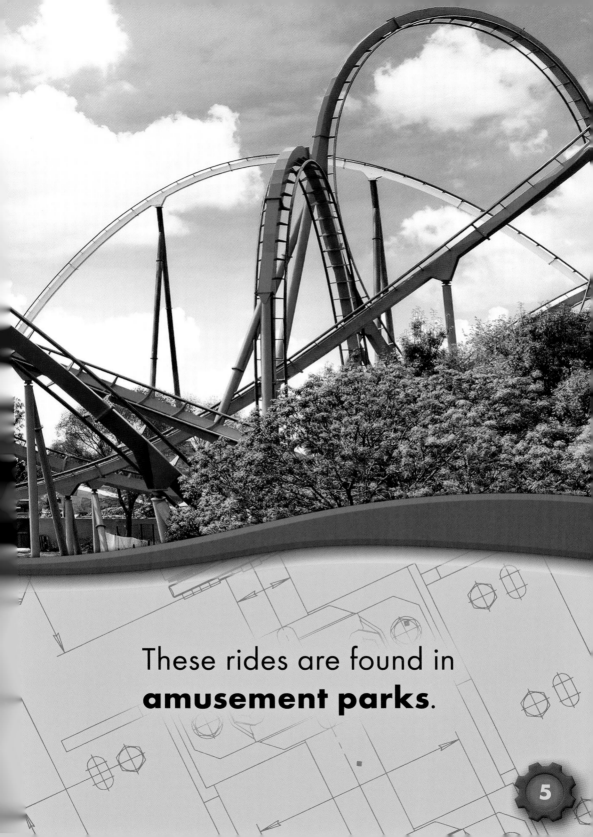

These rides are found in **amusement parks**.

Early roller coasters were large slides covered in ice. People rode sleds down the hill.

Later, tracks were added.
Riders sped down in carts.

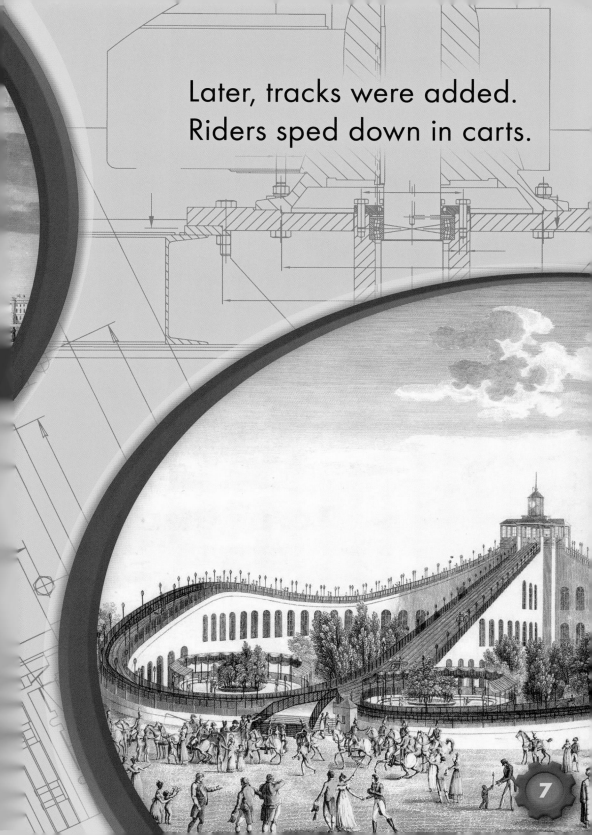

Today, roller coasters
often look like trains.
They have **motors**.

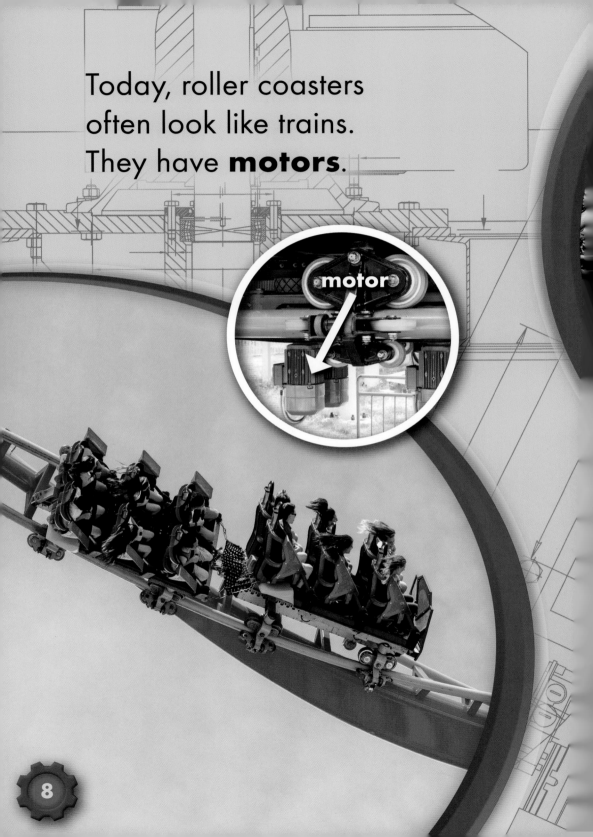

motor

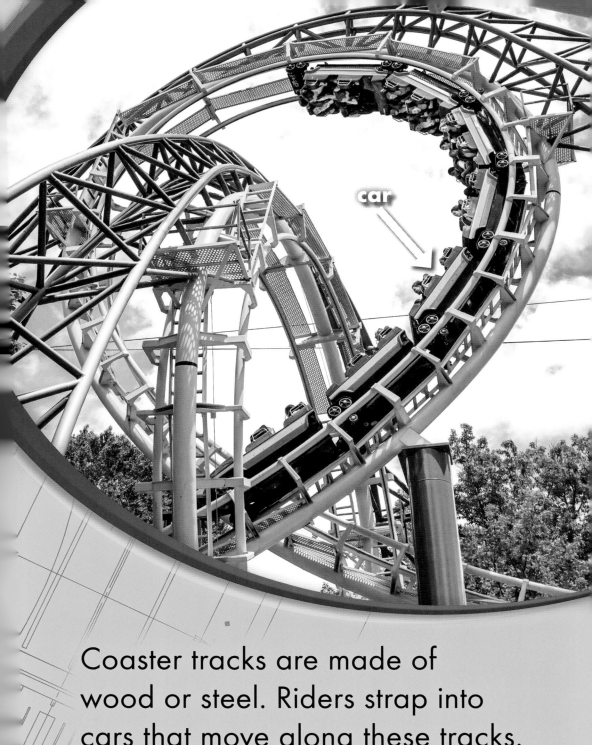

car

Coaster tracks are made of wood or steel. Riders strap into cars that move along these tracks.

Wooden roller coasters usually have rolling hills and wide turns.

10

These coasters offer shaky rides. The track sways as the train of cars rolls over it.

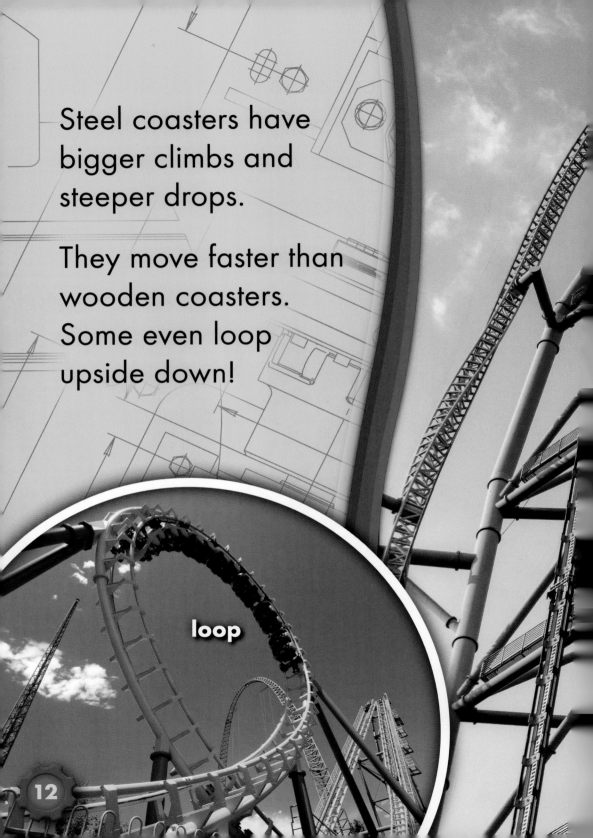

Steel coasters have bigger climbs and steeper drops.

They move faster than wooden coasters. Some even loop upside down!

loop

Kingda Ka

Location: Jackson, New Jersey

Type: steel roller coaster

Year Completed: 2005

Engineer: Intamin Amusement Rides

Height: 456 feet (139 meters)

Top Speed: 128 miles (206 kilometers) per hour

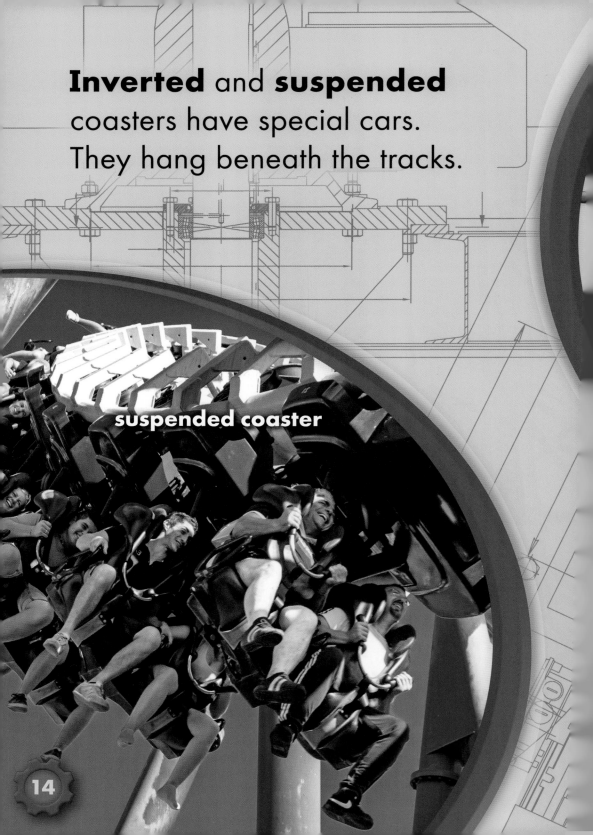

Inverted and **suspended** coasters have special cars. They hang beneath the tracks.

suspended coaster

flying coaster

Flying coasters send riders down the tracks headfirst!

How Do Roller Coasters Work?

A motor often pulls the cars up the first hill. This builds **potential energy**.

Then **gravity** pulls the cars down the drop.

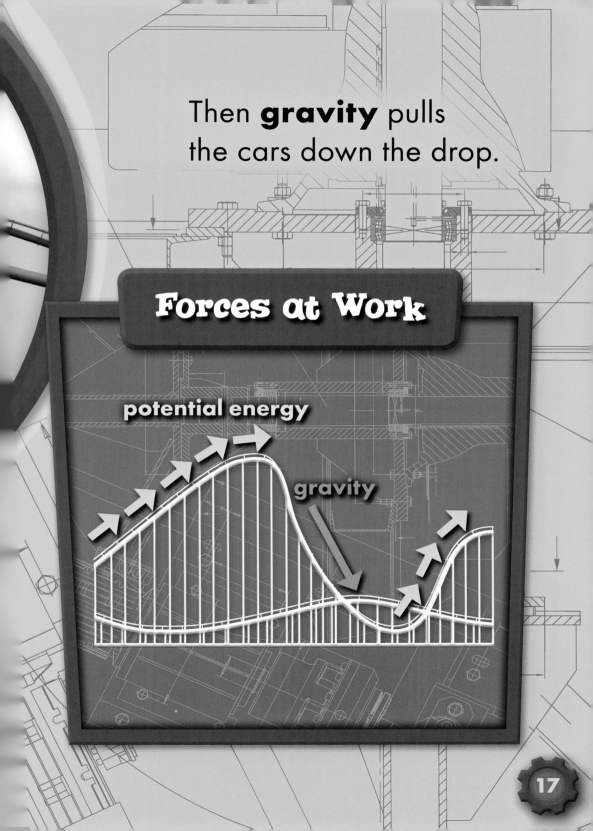

Forces at Work

potential energy

gravity

Forces at Work

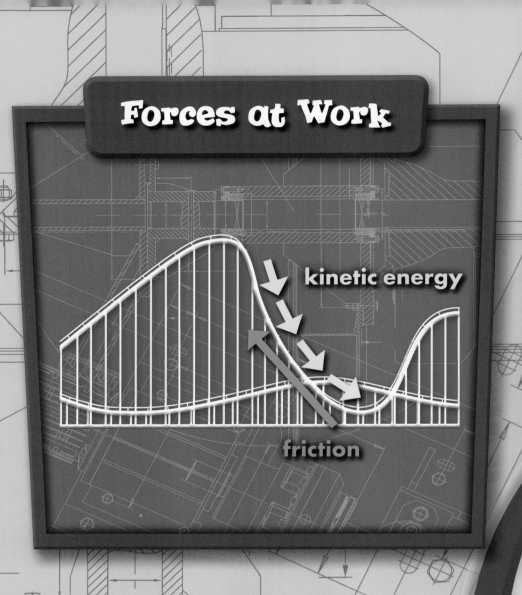

Kinetic energy moves the cars along. Their rolling wheels create **friction** on the track.

Friction helps slow the cars down. **Brakes** bring them to a stop.

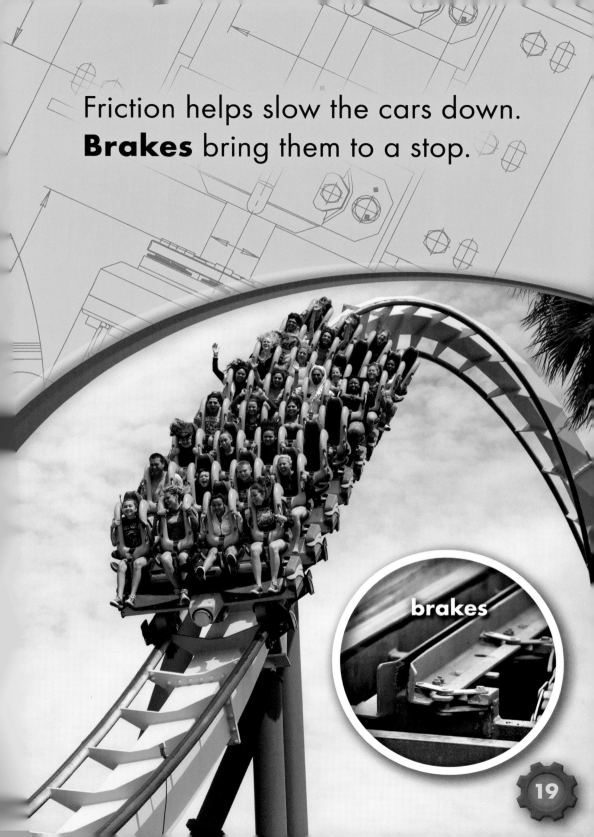

brakes

Some new roller coasters
use **virtual reality**. Riders
travel new worlds while they
speed along the tracks.

These wild rides give
coaster fans a thrill!

Glossary

amusement parks—large areas with rides, food, and games

brakes—machines that slow or stop roller coasters

friction—a force between two objects as they rub against one another

gravity—a force that pulls objects toward the ground

inverted—upside down; inverted roller coasters have cars that run under the tracks.

kinetic energy—moving energy; roller coasters have kinetic energy when they speed down drops.

motors—machines that power roller coasters

potential energy—stored energy; roller coasters have potential energy at the top of hills.

suspended—hanging; suspended roller coasters have cars that run under the tracks and sway from side to side.

virtual reality—a type of computer program that makes users feel like they are in a different place

To Learn More

AT THE LIBRARY

Black, Vanessa. *Kingda Ka Roller Coaster*.
Minneapolis, Minn.: Jump! Inc., 2018.

Kenney, Karen Latchana. *Building a Roller Coaster*.
Mankato, Minn.: Amicus, 2019.

Pettiford, Rebecca. *Roller Coasters*.
Minneapolis, Minn.: Jump! Inc., 2016.

ON THE WEB

Learning more about
roller coasters is
as easy as 1, 2, 3.

1. Go to www.factsurfer.com.

2. Enter "roller coasters" into the search box.

3. Click the "Surf" button and you will see a
   list of related web sites.

With factsurfer.com, finding more information is
just a click away.

Index

The images in this book are reproduced through the courtesy of: Pipochka, front cover; chrupka, front cover; SIHASAKPRACHUM, front cover, pp. 2-3, 22-24; Bubushonok, front cover, pp. 4-24 (blueprint background); darin.k, pp. 4-24 (gears); Brian Kinney, pp. 4-5; Heritage Images/ Getty Images, pp. 6-7; Koller Auktionen/ Wikipedia, p. 7; Cassiohabib, pp. 8, 18-19; flyflyis, p. 8 (inset); Bob Pool, pp. 8-9; George Sheldon, pp. 10-11; Oliver Gerhard/ Alamy, p. 11; Arina P Habich, p. 12; PitK, pp. 12-13; Dmitry V.P, p. 14; Valerii Iavtushenko, pp. 14-15; Vertyr, pp. 17, 18; Byelikova Oksana, pp. 16-17; Seth Michael, p. 19 (inset); Thomas Wagner/ Wikipedia, pp. 20-21.